Lush Dreams, Blue Exile

Fugitive Poems: 1978-1993

George Elliott Clarke

Pottersfield Press,
Lawrencetown Beach, Nova Scotia
1994

Copyright 1994 George Elliott Clarke

All rights reserved. No part of this publication may be reproduced or transmitted in any form or by any means, electronic or mechanical, including photocopying, or by any information storage or retrieval system, without permission in writing from the publisher.

Canadian Cataloguing in Publication Data
    Clarke, George Elliott, 1960-
      Lush dreams, blue exile
      Poems,
      ISBN 0-919001-83-1
    I. Title.
    PS8555.L3748L87 1994 C811'.54 C94-950054-2
    PR9199.3.C53L87 1994

Interior photographs appear courtesy of the Public Archives of Nova Scotia, the National Archives of Canada, Choucri Paul Zemokhol, and Julie Morin.
Back cover photo by Julie Morin.
Cover photo by Ricardo Scipio.
Typeset in 10pt Palatino by Elizabeth Eve.
Printed and bound in Canada

This book was produced with the financial assistance of Multiculturalism Canada — The Secretary of State for Multiculturalism and Citizenship (now the Department of Canadian Heritage).

Pottersfield Press also acknowledges the ongoing support of the Canada Council and the Nova Scotia Department of Tourism and Culture.

Pottersfield Press Ltd.
Lawrencetown Beach
R.R. 2 Porters Lake
Nova Scotia B0J 2S0

To the memory

of

Terrence Bruce Symonds

(1953 - 1990)

and

Miles Dewey Davis III

(1926 - 1991)

Instead of burning, there shall be beauty:
The new spring brandishes fierce, bright blossoms.

Respects

Though they find fresh shelter here, most of these "fugitive" pieces — lyrical lies — appeared in little magazines between 1978 and 1993. Several poems first appeared in *The Windhorse Review*, *The Pottersfield Portfolio*, *The Rap*, *The Fiddlehead*, *Germination*, *Scrivener*, *Matrix*, *Quarry*, *Queen's Quarterly*, *left history*, *The Gargoyle*, *The New Quarterly*, *Imprint*, *Freefall*, *Hudson Valley Echoes (U.S.A.)*, *Nimrod: International Journal of Prose & Poetry (U.S.A.)*, and *Prism International*. A few debuted in the collections, *Sad dances in a field of white*, *American Anthology of Magazine Verse (1985)*, *Ecphore '87 Poetry Anthology*, *Poets 88*, and *Modern Poetry in English*. Twenty-three of these poems premièred in my first book, *Saltwater Spirituals and Deeper Blues* (Porter's Lake, N.S.: Pottersfield Press, 1983). "April in Paris," "April 19, 19__," "April 3-4, 1968," and "Marina: The Love Song of Lee Harvey Oswald" were first issued in *Voices: Canadian Writers of African Descent* (Toronto: HarperCollins, 1992). "April" and "To Say, 'I love you'" are taken from *Provençal Songs* (Ottawa: Magnum Book Store, 1993). Many thanks to the editors and publishers — and to Alexa McDonough, MLA, who quoted "Moses Coady's Sermon" in the Nova Scotian legislature on April 9, 1987 (*Journal of Assembly Debates*).

Friends prepared this text. Choucri Paul Zemokhol sculpted the manuscript. Preston William Chase sounded every word. Allan Garshowitz critiqued several poems in 1983. Elizabeth Eve tended everything. Two lines by Sylvain Garneau are sampled in "Introduction to Modern Languages." Ricardo Scipio disclosed the cover photograph. Margaret Campbell of the Public Archives of Nova Scotia discovered the photographs on pages 8, 12, 56, 68, 70, 76 and 93 (taken by C.R. Brookbank for his 1949 thesis on Africadian communities) as well as those on pages 36 and 45 (taken by Georgia Cunningham). The photograph on pages 30, 34 and 53 are from the National Archives of Canada. C. P. Zemokhol pictured the photograph on page 27. Julie Morin designed the front and back covers, composed the back cover photograph and the photograph on page 90, illuminated the manuscript, and dreamt the title. She has given me sunflowers — in seeds, pictures, and bloom — and blazed for me new directions.

Ah, *Nisan*: Blossoms, snow, lightning.

George Elliott Clarke
Ottawa, *Nisan* 1994

*H*ejiras

Zarahemla	*7*
Gehenna	*11*
Axum-Saba	*35*
Africadia	*51*
I - The Book of Jubilee	*55*
II - Saltwater Spirituals	*69*
III - Deeper Blues	*75*
Sierra Leonia	*89*

Portage

The place names that head each section refer to states of mind, not actual geographies. In the *Book of Mormon*, *Zarahemla* names the Nephite land straddling Bountiful and Desolation. *Gehenna*, a synonym for Hell, alludes to the valley of Hinnom, near Jerusalem, where children were once burned in sacrifice ot Moloch. *Axum* and *Saba* were ancient African-Arabian kingdoms ruled by Queen Saba (*Sheba*), the beautiful Panther-in-the-Blossom. Merging *Africa* and *Acadia* (a word which derives — like *Acadie* — from the Mi'kmaq suffix, *cadie*, which means "abounding in"), *Africadia* signifies Black Nova Scotia, an African-American-founded "nation" which has flourished for more than two centuries. *Sierra Leonia* denotes the African nation which traces its modern origin to the landing of 1,196 Africadian pilgrims in 1792.

    The government of words. And then light. Blue light.

Zarahemla

. . . the whirlwind is our commonwealth.
— Brooks

Salvation Army Blues

      Seeking after hard things —
muscular work or sweat-swagger action —
I rip wispy, Help Wanted ads,
dream of water-coloured sailors
pulling apart insect wings of maps,
stagger down saxophone blues avenues
where blackbirds cry for crumbs.
I yearn to be Ulyssean, to roam
foaming oceans or wrest
a wage from tough, mad adventure.
      For now, I labour language,
earn a cigarette
for a poem, a coffee
for a straight answer,
and stumble, punch-drunk,
down these drawn-and-quartered streets,
tense hands manacled
to snarling pockets.

Primitivism

      He could not escape
the wilderness. Bark
encrusted his wine bottles.
His pencils grew fur
and howled. Sentences
became wild eagles
that flew predatory patterns,
swooping out of a white sky-
page to tear apart field
mice-images, scurrying
for meaning. A carcass-
manuscript rotted on a shelf
or a hillside. He could
not tell the difference.
A bear-trap of ideas
snared him: he could
not poeticize
the country
and not become it;
his poems filling
with neanderthal nudes,
prowling punctuation,
snarling sounds, guttural.

Gehenna

Beauty . . . is like the angel of wrath holding the flaming sword.
— *Fischer*

Coming Into Intelligence

     I understood pain when I was a child,
When black scarves signified Red Baron dash
Or licorice-flavoured savagery
In a no-man's-land of trash and smashed glass
Where torn, dirty pictures sliced open flesh
And kids stoned slow dummies or spat up bugs.
     I understood pain in sketches of war —
The comic-strip striptease of Hitler's War:
I smelt Zyklon-B in lilacs' perfume,
Knew cyanide's almond taste in chocolates,
And bathed in blue crystals like Europe's Jews —
My bathtub flooding with death every night.
     I understood pain; I will not tell lies.
I felt Hiroshima's heat in black ants
Charred to ash by a magnifying glass.
I saw dismemberment in schoolyard art,
Then, in naked, store-window mannequins,
Then, in bodies mired in bombed My Lai roads.
     I understood pain, studied suffering.
I fasted with the bloated innocents
Of Biafra, wept for Kennedy, King.
I confess I did not believe all the blood:
I had been cut only a few times.
Yet, the whole globe oozed a wet, crimson taint.
     I understood pain when I was a child,
When my grandfather, choked by gypsum dust,
Felt his heart seize at light, heave him from darkness.
When I was a child, I was wise,
Knew why we suffer the sorrow we do.
Now that I am a man, I know nothing.

Watercolour for Negro Expatriates in France

      What are calendars to you?
And, indeed, what are atlases?
      Time is cool jazz in Bretagne,
you, hidden in berets or eccentric scarves,
somewhere over the rainbow —
where you are tin-men requiring hearts,
lion-men demanding courage,
scarecrow-men needing minds all your own
after DuBois made blackness respectable.
      Geography is brown girls in Paris
in the spring by the restless Seine
flowing like blood in chic, African colonies;
Josephine Baker on your bebop phonographs
in the lonely, brave, old rented rooms;
Gallic wines shocking you out of yourselves,
leaving you as abandoned
as obsolete locomotives whimpering Leadbelly blues
in lonesome Shantytown, U.SA.

      What are borders/frontiers to you?
In actual seven-league sandals,
you ride Monet's shimmering waterlilies —
in your street-artist imaginations —
across the sky darkened,
here and there, by Nazi shadows,
Krupp thunderclouds,
and, in other places, by Americans
who remind you
that you are niggers,
even if you have read Victor Hugo.
      Night is winged Ethiopia in the distance,
rising on zeta beams of radio free Europe,
bringing you in for touchdown at Orleans;
or, it is strange, strychnine streetwalkers,
fleecing you for an authentic Negro poem
or rhythm and blues salutation.
This is your life —
lounging with Richard Wright in Matisse-green

parks, facing nightmares of contorted
lynchers every night. Every night.

     Scatalogical ragtime reggae haunts the caverns
of *le métro*. You pick up English-language
newspapers and *TIME* magazines,
learn that this one was arrested,
that one assassinated;
fear waking — like Gregor Samsa —
in the hands of a mob;
lust for a black Constance Chatterley,
not even knowing that
all Black people not residing in Africa
are kidnap victims.
     After all, how can you be an expatriate
of a country that was
never yours?

     Pastel paintings on Paris pavement,
wall-posters Beardsley-styled:
you pause and admire them all;
and France entrances you
with its kaleidoscope cafés,
chain-smoking intelligentsia,
absinthe and pernod poets. . . .
     Have you ever seen postcards
of Alabama or Auschwitz,
Mussolini or Mississippi?
     It is unsafe to wallow in Ulyssean dreams,
genetic theories, vignettes of Gertrude Stein,
Hemingway, other maudlin moderns,
while the godless globe
detonates its war-heart, loosing
goose-stepping geniuses
and dark, secret labs.

     Perhaps I suffer aphasia.
I know not how to talk to you.
I send you greetings from *Afrique*
and spirituals of catholic *Négritude*.

        Meanwhile, roses burst like red stars,
a flower explodes for a special sister.
You do not accept gravity in France
where everything floats on the premise
that the earth will rise to meet it
the next day;
where the Eiffel Tower bends over backwards
to insult the Statue of Liberty;
and a woman in the flesh of the moment
sprouts rainbow butterfly wings
and kisses a schizoid sculptor
lightly on his full, ruby lips;
and an argument is dropped over cocoa
by manic mulatto musicians
who hear whispers of Eliot —
or Ellington —
in common prayers.

        You have heard Ma Rainey, Bessie Smith.
You need no passports.
Your ticket is an all-night room
facing the ivory, voodoo moon,
full of Henri Rousseau lions and natives;
and your senses, inexplicably
homing in on gorgeous Ethiopia,
while Roman rumours of war
fly you home.

Five Psalms of Paris

I

A poet thumbs *Gauloise* cigarettes, jabs air
With phrases that don't even speak for him,
Catches *une femme* brandish a voluble
Bottle of cuss, guzzle pure, bootleg jazz,
And fill her mouth with poems that judge every
Lover wanting. *Je veux six francs de vin,
Douze grammes de Zola*, to forget the black
Taste of money and espresso, the black
Odour of love rotting in littered beds,
The brandied smear of prattle and gossip,
The stiletto politics this *Gaulliste*
Practises in splayed and broken *rues*,
Grave with differences, where *littérature*
Is blues skittered across Notre Dame's square.

II

These streetlamps bowed, showered Hitler with light,
When he, in dark *triomphe*, captured these *rues*
His art had missed, light years before, when his
Watercolours had blazed and he had stooped
In damp garrets, to fatten on *Beauty*,
Devouring landscapes like Napoleon.

III

There's a trick with a verb that I'm learning
To do, splintering French and hand language
With *deux Algériens*, whose history
Is frontiers, curried currencies, white sex,
And contraband cigs strong enough to swill.
We watch traffic curve around the *Arche de
Triomphe* like light passed through gravity, like
Colonies pasteurized, bled white, by France.

IV

Dans le café, students drink slow,
Dreaming of Miles Davis and Juliette Greco.

V

In Montmartre, American Vandals,
Bristling with cameras as lewd as missiles,
Slouch by like a dying civilization.
Meanwhile, the sun sluices down backyard plots
Stuffed with roses, shadows, grapes, and lost time.
I crumble cheese, eat apricots, chew dates,
Water everything with apple juice and wine,
While workmen scrape these stones for love. After
The hue and cry of *francs, la Bourse*, damned fools
Trying desperately to keep their coins,
Soon I will taste only oranges and water
Aboard a night train to shrouded *Dunquerque*.

The Death and Life of Garcia Lorca

     Seven Civil Guards bust open his lines,
Crazed black boots spill black ink over his words.
Seven Civil Guards trample *Poetry*.
     They riddle Garcia Lorca in sunlight
In a ditch. Seven bullets score his blood.
He sings, becoming his lyrical works.
     Seven Civil Guards inhume his *corpus;*
Seven Civil Guards now rot, unsung.
But his flesh is song in lovers' rouged mouths.

Guernica

  Crash of rain from a red mouth.
    Scream of blood gripped by a bodiless hand.
    Mouth yelping blackly.

To Liu Chan, Near Nanking

     Liu Chan, bring to us your thin bamboo flute,
A few gold coins pilfered from the market stalls;
Picture the *bourgeoisie* as beasts; accent
Landlords' sharp, rat claws, warlords' hog bellies.
Come with jasmine tea, Mao Zedong proverbs,
To a seeing of answers past answers.
     Liu Chan, cast ballads that pierce like bullets!
Song instills, inspires, infuriates:
The correct notes and the city unfolds;
The right music — the citadel falls.
     Liu Chan, my storm-muscled men, pitched below
With captured oranges, cashmere, and poets
Dreaming strategy, cherries, concubines,
Cry for songs to arm the broken peasants.
     Blood is crimson, our red banners bloody.
Is this what stops you? Sing, Liu Chan! Or die.

Mao Inks "The People's Liberation Army Captures Nanking"

- a lu shih
April 1949

    Seizing the mountain, this crazy, jagged
Zigzag of crags, snow cliffs, cleft, skittish rocks
Lunging toward the moon's white gravity,
I imagine dragons' wings brush my head.
I push vertically, hear the sky break,
Level the old order of things.
    Below, the state totters. My million troops,
Their hands blood-baptised, their heads flame-haloed,
Scribe fresh history with spent shells and hymns.
The city unscrolls, awaits our crimson
Calligraphy, brush-stroke and sword-stroke.
Look! Snow hammers earth with leaden softness. . . .
Ah, this world's mutable: mountains become coral reefs.

Marina: The Love Song of Lee Harvey Oswald

     Here are some early narcissus for your blue eyes,
Marina Prusakova.
Let's mosey beside the River Minsk—you, nineteen and perfect,
And I just twenty-one.
Look, in still life, Father Lenin smiles upon us.
Take these blue plums and some hot, black tea.
     I've scribbled in my Historic Diary
About the workers's Zion — sunlight gilding
Birch branches and hydroelectric towers,
Illuminating everything, everything.
I promise you we'll blind history.
Taste these sweet plums, Marina.
     Let's dawdle in doorways while fresh snow mills:
This world is like a coming storm.
Peasants will toss flowers while our steamer vanishes,
Silver narcissus petals snow through air,
When we embark for glimmering America
To become its shining President and First Lady.

November 22, 1963

A woman teeters up the slanted street,
Screams, "The president's been shot!", collapses,
Her face jigsawed by tilting lines and tears.
The gold, late autumn air slumps to the earth.
Leaves snap from branches, branches snap from trees.
I, a boy, just shaken from my last nap,
Stand at my home's door, watch our neighbour weep.
I tremble, clench my mother's long skirt.
She pulls me against her thigh to protect me.
Her warm hand shields my head against early
Snow or knowledge, but I have just found fear.
I expect this world cools, darkens, with age.

The Martyrdom of El Hajj Malik El Shabazz

     Like bees scenting the myrrh and frankincense
Of his flesh, bullets congregate around him;
Blood honeys at the exit wounds in his heart.
Smoke — the nepenthe of his own sweet death — staggers him;
He falls, becoming a garden of perfume.
     The faithful swathe him in ivory muslin,
But his flesh goes further, straining into starlight.

Vallière's **Nègres blancs d'Amérique**

      Duplessis grins and stuffs the bags of Yank
Bankers with Québec's iron ore, gold, and pride.
He leers from every tabloid and billboard
And pours hydro into New England's mills.
My friends drown in *brasseries dégueulasses*
Or blow out their brains in bullet-pocked woods
After prostituting lovers for fresh
Water, after watching their bastards die.
      Sick of the coma of silence that numbs
Mon pays in its stupid cupidity,
I steel my faith—bitter as Gaspé seas,
Black as Alma rocks, cold as Rouyn winters.
Listen, Trudeau, theft can have bankers' hands —
And oppression a bishop's smiling, holy face.
It's not enough to preach of liberty.
To abolish slavery, first smash chains!

April 3-4, 1968

    A century of rain smoulders in luscious,
Stark richness. He meccas through wet lightning
To the church to chant his death. He feels sparks,
Something torching the tindered, fissile air.
To the pulpit, he ascends, thundering
Justice, Jesus, and John, because God
Has mapped The Promised Land; his voice splinters,
Lightning rives the rapt church:
I've been to the mountaintop. Tomorrow,
After the rain, he steps into the cool
Dusk, into the cool, wet, Tennessee dusk.
    Andy dreams he hears an engine crackle.
Ralph jumps *instinctively*, then turns, then turns,
And sees King, his arms outstretched, blood blazing
From the hole the bullet's punched through his neck.

The Assassination of Robert F. Kennedy

The senator's form fleshes the still-life
Traced in white chalk on the chill, pantry floor.
Television telescopes his posture
To a single limited edition.
Artists copy his model agony,
While Kennedy, reclined like pale Marat —
Stabbed in his bath — stiffens on a cold slab.
Reporters illustrate the classic grief —
A widow's flowers, the arc the bullet drew
Through dream and desire — while the subject fades
To oblivion, blacks out like Hanoi
At night, pummeled by the mortar of stars.

October Crisis

      All this hurt night, police clatter through *rues*
Constricted by their fears, and splash through glass,
Wade through sawdust doors, to handcuff lovers
And strip-search their fat, suspicious tomes,
Mistaking *cubisme* for *communisme*,
And beat down the *fleur de lys* with truncheons,
And place moans of broken French in smashed mouths —
Innocents *blessé* by *Crime*-blessèd cops.
      Now Liberals quote slick, quisling Latin
To each other in the gun-hushed Commons,
Softening, with suave, veronal accents,
And allusions to Montesquieu and Locke,
The filthy, guttural blows of gloved fists,
Their unapprehended insurrection.

The Assassination of Indira Gandhi

      In Kitchener, Hallowe'en frost chokes roses,
The spruce gangrene, and haystacks flame in fields
Where Mennonites preach black, scorched-earth gospels.
Children, invented for death, slouch to school.
Mourning editors inter last night's remains:
"Paying the fine of worldly existence,
Mrs. Gandhi died, freed in her rose garden."
I dream only the brown mother dropping
Among roses, azaleas, bullet casings,
The dark harvest of scarlet Amritsar,
The Golden Temple crimsoned by her troops.
      Now, the pitched heavens smell of orange blossoms,
Petrol, for her body fuses flowers
And fire, and chars to incense for Shiva,
Buddha, Allah, all the incensed gods,
And New Delhi burns with skin of savaged Sikhs
And bone-white stars flung across tar-pit skies.
Gandhi's been mangled by History's claws;
But now, being scent, she's freed by wind
And waves to float far from this wet, red world
Where many weep and gnash their teeth and smash
Their neighbours' brains with rocks or clubs.

Judas: A Biography

       You sported the silks that Christ never wore —
A svelte, scarlet tie for every white suit,
And pounded your Bible to press your points.
Your mouth crammed with fine words, you hymned sermons
That moved the poor to sign over welfare cheques.
When you paraded, macho, in tight jeans,
And strangled guitars, thin, nubile debs wept
And wrung their tear-soaked hair upon your feet.
       Then, still greedy, you hawked dry snow — cocaine —
And gulled and pimped tender, small-breasted girls.
When Mary, your fine whore, quit you for Christ,
You raged: Blood beat in your skull like a drum.
You had Christ jailed, crowned with barbed-wire, shocked,
Then strung with piano wire from a lamppost.

Axum-Saba

*Awake, O north wind; and come, thou south;
blow upon my garden, that the spices thereof may flow out.
— Song of Solomon 4:16*

The Annunciation

    God's seeded Mary but Joseph ain't sure,
And rounds on Mary, his hands — muscled knots.
He slaughters the cardtable, brains china,
Yanks up a protesting, hand-tooled chair
And batters it into kindling. How could
His Sabbath School teacher be so two-faced?
His hair psycho, his clothes shocked, he swears blood,
Bawls to deaf sidewalks to swallow him up.
    But Mary's carrying a young truth who heals;
She doesn't need Joseph, only his love.
She runs to calm him while leaves catch fire.

After Marx

The salesgirl arranges jewels
in the shop window —
unaware
she herself is a jewel.

Love Poem / Song Regarding Weymouth Falls

      At the *Six-Hiboux*, where the Acadian
and the Micmac saw the six scholar-birds
whose insomnia is natural,
probably a million moons ago;
at the Sissiboo River, where it kisses
wetly Saint Mary's Bay and fans on out
into brown Fundy tides shimmering
like a new world Nile;
this is where the world as we know it begins,
all blue and beguiling,
all because of her who homes with the pines,
so elegant, evergreen, egalitarian —
richly female. . . .

      At the homeless highway, where it waits
and wails asphalt anthems of hit-and-run
before plunging wildly into woods whispering
Kejimkujik songs of she I love in blossom notes
of the most crimson and pleasant apples
and the fattest calves of the land,
there is built Weymouth Falls
and its African Baptist church
and its antique lumberyard
and the dwelling of her I take time
to make time with. . . .

      Ah, delirious delight is mine! — the careless
debauchery of stars bearing only good luck/
glad tidings; the sweet desolation of distance,
ebbing and flowing; drunken joy
of violent youth, violently in love,
as she moves to apex of my cosmos;
and the old, troubled world wheels around her,
song pours itself through my flesh,
drives me to her gravity-field of beauty,
even to the edge of the Sissiboo,
hand-in-hand with her.

A Poem with the Single Title of "Desire"

      You salt away my green, tender letters
To cure — or decay — in forgetfulness.
There, foxed by tears, the dark sheen of words
Will fade slowly to blurs, my Negro blush
Of eloquence corrode to white silence.
Starved for air, my love poems'll coarsen, stiffen
Into stark, crude, Anglo-Saxon stresses
That'll hinder, screw, all pronunciation.
      S., how will your beauty appreciate
If left unsung?
                I'll wrench poems from branches,
Scribble your name in the waterfall's noise,
And make all *Nature* our rose-embroidered
Canticles, to give this dark-complected love
A hearing.
      Them that have ears, they will hear.

Violets for Your Furs

I still dream the steamed blackness, witness, of you in rain;
I talk about that — pouring living fire on guitar strings,
And suffer Cointreau's blues aftertaste of burnt orange,
The torturous bitter flavour of the French in Africa,
The crisis of your long black hair assaulting your waist,
Your small, troubling breasts not quite spoken for,
Your spontaneous mouth unconsummated with kisses,
'Cos you cashed in your pretty *Négritude* and gone.

Ah, you were a living *S*, all Coltrane or Picasso swerves;
Your hair stranded splendid on the gold beach of your face,
So sweet, I moaned black rum, black sax, black moon,
The black trace of your eyelash like lightning,
The sonorous blackness of your skin after midnight —
The sadness of loving you glimmering in Scotch.
Now, this sheet darkens with the black snow of words;
In my sheets, a glimpse of night falls, then loneliness.

I can't sleep — haunted by sad sweetness outside the skull,
The hurtful perfume you bathed in by the yellow lamp,
Three-quarters drunk, your rouged kiss branding my neck,
The orange cry of my mouth kindling your blue night skin.
The night blossoms ugly, I down gilded damnation.
I've been lovin' you — more than words — too long to stop now.
What will happen next? I can't know, you should know:
The moon tumbles, caught in fits of grass, seizures of leaves.

April in Paris

    I wander among the graves of poets,
Stalk inspiration with a loaded pen,
And collect bunches of fresh, cold lilies.
I exult in sprays of green — vines and leaves
Vaulting over walls, whelming *avenues* —
But brood as *une beauté* peels a broadsheet
From keeling wind; the sky sketches elm nudes.
    I can't stop thinking of you, so lovely,
Rambling the ramparts of the *Citadelle
De Québec.* I yearn to drape you in silks,
Array you in gaudy blue-and-white flags.
    If you will offer me another home —
A balcony where I may type this poem —
I will bring you wine and albescent honey.
I'll name you with the most beautiful nouns:
Carnation, orchid, rose, iris, trillium, anemone.

Introduction to Modern Languages

The best part of our lives we are wanderers in Romance....
— Bridges

      Once I cast you as a Tahitian,
using "auburn," "melon," and "sandals"
all in one poem. That was years ago,
when we hiked to the prof's house in the country,
among autumn apples, scudding leaves,
woodsmoke tincturing clear, October air.
I'd sat beside you at the Shakespeare play
that day in Stratford,
in delicate darkness,
loving even then how your hair fell.
      The next October, your quick steps clattered
over the narrow, cobbled streets of Québec,
coming down to meet my train at midnight,
coming down to meet my train at midnight,
because my letters were much too lonely,
their ink was tears you could see.
      You fried an omelette with ham and green pepper
and jimmied red wine from the cramped fridge.
The rain flared into snow because it had to —
the temperature would not remain neutral.
Leaves marshalled and assaulted the wind.
We straggled through Québec with a Latin text
composed in French, and lollygagged
in your narrow apartment to glimpse
the evasive, ivory moon — and. . . .
Autrefois, le soir, au bord de l'extase,
Je t'amenais et nous nous aimions.
      Waterloo was so far away from where we were,
no one knew what we were up to. I kept
slicing pens into silent paper
to spy meaning pour from utter clarity.
I still demonstrate my love that way —
in a *langue* only you must understand.

April 19, 19__

      He was faltering under the pressure of love;
his blood gelled slowly into honey:
nectar was accumulating in his veins.
Becoming fiercer and fiercer for her, his measures
broke up sonnets because they couldn't accomodate
the vast, exhaustless pleasure of her kiss.
      Troubadours and toreadors cried of her all night
so he couldn't sleep. Her name quarried *corrida*
and *querida*. Was she born in silk?
Some liquid, icy fire chilled her skin,
inciting her nerves to moan at the caress.
Her kisses were rain upon his face.
      He brought her lilies and the bluesiest
albas ever strummed by a Nova Scotian,
yielding their private language to a public form,
because of the night she lay beside him
and the day they lolled in apple blossoms.
They were guilty of unspeakable love.
      There was the beginning and that only:
the first poem that made her gasp; the first embrace
that made him echo a millenium of songs
by entombed, regretful poets who wished
they had known lips as mauve and lush as hers.
Their love survives now only in this poem.

For K. C. O.

      After mean years of mosquitoes, bogs, thorns,
When doubt meant a sour bout of Scotch to forget
What I dared not forget — my field of rest,
My love, our green and wild bed wet by tears,
When night poured oblivion into my skull,
Crows gathered force to break and enter dreams,
And I thought I slept on barbed-wire or nails,
K. O., your wheat hair is sweet to me now.
      I've known the eastward rush of trains bearing
Love's cords—the cut and measured guitars of trees;
Now, you're golden hair and lush hazard,
Lovely danger, a constant, stammered blues
I can barely mumble or dare to sing,
A happiness I can't stop remembering.

En Lutte!

     In the night café, A. perches nun-like,
Quaffs beer that's "sweat of Québecois workers,"
Catechizes on farmers, class martyrs,
The rococo hellfire of surplus value,
Envisions a blood-red dawn of banners.
Her pointed eyes and mouth, agape with fire,
Attract; her shape's Marxist strictness recalls
Saint Joan of Arc; her dark, Catholic hair
Makes a confessional of her white face.
     She trounces Trotsky while stars come and go;
Then, her sermon done, she troops into dawn,
Her red cape inflaming light. I follow
Her slenderness, not the Party's harsh line,
Wanting her love more than revolution.
She senses my lack of discipline,
Calls down hell on all "imperialists."
But I dream of making poems from bread and roses,
Holding her small, white fists that pound tables.

April

Crocuses blanch and blush and push
through decadent, fainting snow
like peasants storming the Bastille.

White winds turn pages slowly into leaves;
leaden water disfigures, crushes the creek.

You wake and shake your glinting hair —
sable lightning splintering our pillow. *Ce matin,
tu ressembles à une demoiselle d'Avignon.*

Now, the crocuses flaunt rich, carnal perfumes;
and the April trees incandesce with blossoms.

To Say, "I love you"

To say, "I love you,"
"je t'aime" —
your white thigh chafing my brown
in our beautiful sleep
and lovetoil,
the taking and giving,
your mouth
on mine —
the wet lustre
of our lips and sexes
becomes silver oiling,
burnishing,
dull, usual words;
French and English gleam
with fresh meaning:
leaf-sifted light
soleils, shadows,
our bared love.

Africadia

*Go down, Moses,
way down in Egypt land,
Tell old Pharaoh
to let my people go.*
— Spiritual

Testament

Out of the bitter sea, I come, raging the faith of the Beautiful Ones who broke from chains and bastard tongues to hymn the insurrectionist spirituals —those home-made songs culled from potato patch, hog farm, or stony beach, those Bible-beauty songs plucked from apple trees and guitars. So this is my testament, be it smoke and blood; this is my gospel, be it longing and sorrow. This is my book of songs, echoing the desire of all those who stand on the bouldered shores of the North Atlantic, looking eastward, ever dreaming, ever wanting.

East Coasting

For Boyd Warren Chubbs

Poets sigh this land's brogue
its beach-broken speech . . .

Wharves slouch in fog,
tractors slump in fields.

Butterflies issue
from dark chambers of fruit.

Skeletons people these white fields.

I-The Book of Jubilee

*The Spirit of Slavery never seeks refuge
in the Bible of its own accord. . . .
It vaults over the sacred enclosures,
and courses up and down the Bible,
seeking rest and finding none. . . .
It flies from light into the sun,
from heat into devouring fire;
and from the voice of God
into the thickest of his thunders.
— John William Robertson*

Invocation of the Prophet

     After cells, traps, slaveday terrors in Tidewater Sodom,
after lashings, brandings, lynchings, Virginian Egypt,
after bastard night and black laws,
I came, Richard Preston, God-called
Apostle of Liberty,
to this earth dreaming wood, wind, and water gods,
to this birchbark Canaan, to this Nova Scotia.
     And I came, spiritualized by cornhusker poets,
hollering melody from rivers and rocks,
pulling rhythm from ploughs and earth,
finding words in hoes, whores, horses,
the chink, clink, of chains,
the apple brandy slur-speech of horseback preachers . . . .
     And I came, drawn by a fiery faith,
so that not all be frozen in idolatry,
but some saved fierily,
their combustion sparking a flaming church,
a true New Light chapel,
illuminating dark world and Heaven.
     These pages record my acts,
committed, oh committed, now to fire —
even to burn future hearts.

— Halifax, 1854

Portents

      At my birth,
scarecrow priests grimaced,
sickle-lightning reaped black rampikes,
blood spattered corn,
haystacks burst into hills of fire.
One old man saw white angels
and black angels battle in a skull-white sky;
another understood and explained.
My mother wailed to know such pain,
greater than love, yet love.
      But when I was withdrawn,
oh, into the shrouded night,
the sick cabin near collapse,
the murmuring, prophesying wind,
the wild-minded ministers seeing things,
I cried not.

Signs

      I saw the seagull, saint of harbours,
grey pier-prophet, miles inland,
burning but not burning.
I eyed a book of stone through water-light:
its words moved when read,
scattering like tadpoles;
yet, I was not deceived.
I prophesied droughts from leaf-equations,
deciphered hymns to resurrect rain.
      Some scoffed, but I had heard
a Royal voice, from screaming air,
peal, "This is your duty,
you are called to do;
rough or hewn, you must bear it."
Then, Christ's great arms,
extended as on the cross,
crossed out the blood-black horizon.

Autobiography

     Out of one womb and into another,
into the world and out of my mother,
to blue-white water and grey boulders,
I came, thirsting.
     In that driftpine desert,
I divined rain, swilled rum from the mouths
of women (smoked molasses,
wet, under stars),
but thirsted still.
     I scrabbled among book-stones,
wandered, parched, the Annapolis-appled world,
then saw the ocean crimson with blood
at sunset, and, drinking,
was satisfied, was born
to a new heaven and a new earth.

Evangelist

      Crows crack a white, porcelain sky,
carve one fine, black line;
through the fracture, some light
falls, filters, but little.
      Beneath that pale plate,
I was pressed, flattened,
made weary, the same as everyone,
my gospel-fire fainting.
      Then, I found a few believers,
forest boards, and stoked a bonfire-church
in the name of God and the old songs
no other church would sing.
      We dark ones joined,
becoming incendiary,
one vast conflagration unto God.

Scripture

      Shadowed rivers shirring into light,
sky bruising purple-black,
apple trees shivering in icy winds —
all of sacred, free *Nature* authors
our sermons, prayers, hymns.
Every Bible word literal,
every letter law:
      In the beginning, maples
and willows, pleached,
offered natural chapels,
when earth was not grave,
but bright green grove.
      Now, we must build
our means of mating
Heaven and earth.

Sermon

  Homing gulls compose
canticles of light and shadow
above our heads and hearts
too attached to gravity.
  We would be nearer Heaven
if wings were ours, we believe;
but, no: land, earth, humble us —
we rise from soil, then return,
sinking through broken twigs and fog,
finally to lend our substance
to mushrooms and earthworms,
completing the ordained circle.
  Seek not God on the wing;
knowing our farness from Him,
He hath descended to us this moment.
  Amen.

Work

      Across orchard country *amlamkook*,
ox-carts, heaped with rainy hay,
creak noisily from marshes.
Fieldhands — ochre angels, sepia saints —
creep across a crazy, sagging bridge,
become mere, moving lights.
      I suffer an immaculate image:
an inshore church, lighthouse, a fiery home,
leaping into flame-vision
out of the tinder of Thy tenderness,
the kindling of Thy love —
a holocaust of roses,
an inferno of white wood.

Drought

      A peck of corn, a pint of salt:
our rations.
A withered, hungry horse
stands in need of prayer.
The heavens marble,
refuse rain.
What ashen faith
a dream dried to dust produces...
      Oh Lord, remember me, Thy servant!
Stretch forth Thine arms across
the firmament, fertilize the clouds.
Oh, for I am more desolate
than an abandoned homestead,
more desolate
than a burnt-out church.

Granville Mountain

After the glare and fire
of sunrise water in a creek
where cattle shimmer in living sacrifice;
after this ritual and others—
water-lily, blazing sunflowers,
illuminating the Annapolis River;
after ruminating of rocks and clefts,
and chanting the prayer of exile
and the lover's cry,
guttural songs,
I toil up Granville Mountain,
guided by a secret, silent voice,
and, burning in the sun,
standing at stony summit,
proclaim, oh hosanna, oh hallelujah,
the African Baptist Association.

Christ Church

To Septimus Clarke

    The holy mountains reverberate
with fish and lumber barker cries
and campaign promises,
and glint in sunlight and fog.
    Withdrawn now, awaiting
translation to my scourged nation again,
I see the Africans of *Megumaage* established
in Christ church, true church, Baptist church,
ablaze with spirit, each member
a pentecostal flame.
I see rural chapels dazzling white,
prayers requited.
    No matter now, death or destiny,
I have other fires to bank.
I go. This record?
    Go tell it on the mountain.
Go sound the Jubilee.

II - Saltwater Spirituals

*God has not gone to some distant star,
He's in the fields where the toilers are.*
— Spiritual

The Sermon on the Atlantic

      Fishers float above
blue earth and death,
and lower lines insect-angels
ascend and descend, bringing
peace to priest amphibians,
slithering in a hungry world.
      Fishers let down these lines
to rescue those unwilling to be saved,
but who will greedily
seize the angled offer, and be yanked,
bleeding crimson froth at mad,
shocked-open mouths, now protesting
feverishly, upwards into heaven's
cold, blinding air.

Hammonds Plains African Baptist Church

    Drunk with light,
I remember maritime country.
I cry Birchtown blues, the stark,
sad beauty of this Kimmerian land.
    I dream of a faithful dory
battling the blue, cruel combers
of a feral, runaway ocean —
a Trotskyite ocean in permanent revolution —
turning fluid ideas over and over
in its leviathan mind,
turning driftwood, drums, and conundrums
over and over. . . .
    Then, crazy with righteous anger,
I think of Lydia Jackson,
slave madonna, soon rich with child,
whose Nova Scotian owner,
the distinguished Dr. Bulman,
kicked her hard in the stomach,
struck her viciously with fire tongs,
and then went out upon the ocean
in his dory
to commune with God.

Campbell Road Church

      At Negro Point, some forgot sleep
to spy the fire-and-brimstone sun
blaze all gold-glory
over a turquoise harbour
of half-sunken, rusted ships,
when it was easy to worship
Benin bronze dawns,
to call "hosanna" to archangel gulls. . . .
But none do now.
      Rather, an ancient CN porter lusts
for Africville —
beautiful Canaan of stained glass and faith,
now limbo of shattered glass and promises,
rats rustling like a mayor's robe.
      He rages to recall
the gutting death of his genealogy,
to protest his home's slaughter
by homicidal bulldozers
and city planners molesting statistics.
      At Negro Point, some forgot sleep,
wailed, "Oh freedom over me,"
heard mournful trains cry like blizzards
along blue Bedford Basin. . . .
      None do now.

Fall River Church

     A steamer-tractor parts
a shifting sea, churning the thick,
dry earth near broken horses
that flounder in dust,
gasp for grass,
drown.
     Soon, some saint will find them,
floating in the Sargasso drought,
jettisoned from care like sick
or dead slaves,
and he will cast out a net —
like one who founds a church —
to rescue those flailing,
to bury deeper those sunken.

III- *Deeper Blues*

*Was no money to make in them days.
You would make a couple of dollars a day,
that's all, was no money.
You made money
only to make the next fellow rich.
— John Crawley, aged 94,
East Preston, Africadia, 1982.*

Hinterland

    To you, it is no mystery —
a creature-crazy asylum
where wood-wild lumberjacks fly
off at the axe handle,
scour black bush thick with things,
where mosquito-words
draw blood, not pictures,
terrifying the dying daylights
out of you.
    Your city is where you think
real things happen:
new streetlamps coming into existence
to expunge human shadows,
artists forging their names
from street signs and obscurity,
nuns saving none
from brick and Buick suicide.
It is the home of the national,
natural culture —
monomanic music,
zero gravity grope-dance.
    For you do not believe true
these sea chanty towns
where totem lightpoles spire fire to God,
artists brandish tomahawk-tints
in the wild, paint brush country,
and western eastern cowboys
emerge from the dark undergrowth
of guitars and twang godawful gospels
in tangle-taverns and bramble-bars,
far, far from your city circle — the concentric,
constraining, strangling rings
of mobsters and millionaires.
    You do not recognize
aboriginal art:
fishers who are magicians, who snatch
shimmering cod
out of silver, slippery air.
    Hinterland is that country
you cannot even begin
to imagine.

Homage to the Beloved Country

The grief-stricken sun plummets
into the lattice-work of pines and spruce,
and as it crumples into dusk,
its light falls crooked and bent on earth
as it is in water.
      I witness its collapse and know tragedy:
how a dream of freedom can be twisted into dust
by a narrow and naked land.
      Still, there is the fiery, ebon beauty
of Aberdeen Angus and new ewes;
the renaissance of a root and a name
granted by the New Light chapels
of a cow and two sheep
in *this* world; and, suddenly,
I lust for the meat of apples
and the drink of rain,
a saviour not nailed down
to a cruciform of certainty,
and to fly my love on wings of corn
over a sky of meadow —
to have the fat years follow these thin.

Hymn for Portia White

The white, bathing moon
    ogles itself in the sea,
        all black and handsome.

J. M. W. Turner's Nova Scotia

    Miraculous how light raptures,
Roots, in water,
Transmutes to holy morning colours —
Chlorophyll, cobalt, and copper,
A wash of greens, a spray of petals,
Upon pale china canvas
Or, if caught in brooks,
Flashes into fish.
    Yet, all blanches or blackens,
Withers or rots, with revelation.
Soon will dawn a darkling moon —
So white, it deceives many,
So white, it evades vision,
Not light but light's reflection.

Moses Coady's Sermon

I - Declaration

Old, gnarled, broke, with eye-patch and cane, I spy
The moon get high and holy, tell farmers —
With dirt ground right in their linen, to live
By grit. And I shout the resurrection
Of those who vote, get voted down, who see
Mountains fall in a dawn of flames, whose wives
Suffer thinness of gruel and waists even
After childbirth. I call for hogs and hope,
Rural basics, the good presents, because
Freedom means not having to die for things.

II - Death of John McKay

Never mind the aquamarine night, clouds
Breaking for alms of moon, *Beauty*
Is a moaning misery in this land:
Trees slap like whips; washing lines screech; blown soil
Clogs rooms. The wind rumours John McKay's death;
His last tears shine in his wife's public tears.
A farmer, he made the world green; but, first,
Cape Breton coal dust hollowed out his lungs.
His grave twists speech to silence at my mouth.
But silence cannot be my friend: my love
Condemns this crazy, provisional world
That cheats and robs its citizens of each
Other, that starves the poor to stuff the rich:
Hunger's the limit of its liberty.

Song of Ecclesiastes

      The wind chooses where song should fall,
Where chaff should drift. The wind decides.
The wind plunges toward the south,
Then lunges again unto the north.
The wind sifts sand through windows,
Snow through black ash branches,
Cold rain through graves and fields.
The wind chooses, the wind decides.

Peggy's Cove

       In pitched night fog, I stagger upon *Fear* —
Cabals of rock, wreckage, sobs of wet death,
Caterwauled epics of drowning, a salt
Nightmare — this dun, Expressionist Stonehenge
Of hunched and broken anarchic boulders
Heaped against the fierce, mad, dark Atlantic
By homicidal force that drove them there
In dumb, impaling anger. I tremble;
A blind roar suffocates the stars, a black
Hatred lathers this grotesque beach and howls.
I hear groanings like bones being smashed — and cries
Like infants hurled head-first against brick walls.

Taunt's Hill

For Chester Jarvis

      T. hooks his bass, slits it open: wet notes
Spill out like guts, bloodying night with blues.
He moans over almond-tinctured Leafy,
Wonders when she'll, if she'll . . . then breaks for rum,
Hollars out for "mo' molasses lasses,"
Then keens a black, saltwater elegy
For O., whose stomach leaked over gravel
After the worming bullet burrowed home,
And the attorney-general, white liar,
Crawled into the papers and laughed like that,
Letting the assassin piss on O.'s bones.
      I remember T. like a smile, that thin
Poet of Alcoholics Anonymous,
Who fretted over Ang in the N. S.,
Back when my engine hurt, coughing up weeds,
And Haney's grassfire went loco, turning
His three-generation, pinewood home to snakes.
Queen Anne's lace fans over the foundations.
      Last April, nigh spring, T. fell in his chair
While snow heaved and heaved against his window;
He remembered the dead among their corn.
Rum blazed while temperatures went arctic,
Chopped wood faltered in his stove. A blizzard
Hacked an icy path through his brain:
He was climbing Taunt's Hill—at last.

Halifax Blues

    Junked cars bunch, hunch like rats; laundry,
Lynched, dangles from clotheslines; streetlamps sputter,
Gutter, blow out; gross, bloated cops
Awake and pummel Lysol-scented drunks,
While God grins at scabbed girls who scour the streets
To pass pestilence to legislators.
    The harbour crimps like a bent, black cripple;
It limps, drops dead on rocks: each wave's a crutch
That's pitilessly kicked aside. Above,
Grim gulls beat night with wings that beat back rain.
    I drag poems from the water's muffled black.
They chomp, wriggle, and thrash on *Love*'s bloody,
Two-pronged hook. I slap them, writhing still,
On paper, and cry beautiful darkness —
The baroque scream of a feeling. Hurt crows
Caw my sorrow better than a thousand white
Doves. I skulk beneath these fainting streetlamps
To disturb taverns, set cops ill at ease.

2641 Fuller Terrace

        Gilly uplifts his gothic blues guitar
To black voice, yowls like rum-fired ice cracking
In a full glass, and stammers, "Jealous Love,"
"Two-Timing Love," and "Bad, Low-Down, Filthy Love."
His felt weight shakes his skeleton; he squints
Into deliberate, welcomed darkness,
His fingers stroking strings tensed like fine bones:
He knows the steeled softness of some lovers.
        He vents Bob Marley's poem, "Waiting in Vain,"
Practically weeping the passionate words,
I don' wanna wait in vain for yo' love,
Accompanied by eloquent guitar,
Then the sad, subtropical saxophone
Of John Coltrane, who eyes this blues genius
From a black-and-white photograph that fronts
The thirty-one days of January.

Surah LXXVII—The Emissaries

Red apples and brown coffee
in indigo insurgency:
paired, dark forms of ducks,
moving in water,
seem like strange rocks
or the breasts of my daughter —
while the rotary develops
images of autos and donut shops.

A motel sign glares blood-red
opposite a home for the newly dead.
The black body of a Bible,
lynched on the pine of a table,
is as motionless as possible.
I would read it if I were able
(if its words were not birds of prey
in a war-tinted sky, khaki and grey).

Coin-operated lovers
exchange lucre in cold covers.
Piercing lights of moloch lamps
hurl arrows of electricity
to herald darkness where it camps
in the stock markets of the city.
I would alter if there were change
to alter what is not pre-arranged.

I have lost so much of what was nothing
(even the stars above the lakes are frothing).
Have I said that my daughter's breasts
are like two young, black swans —
that each generation of emptiness rests
upon my toiling for such futile funds?
I go forth mornings to keep alive
the human dream, the human drive.

Crying the Beloved Country

      Why can I not leave you
like a refugee?
Reluctantly, I abandon
your sea-bound beauty,
shale arms and red clay lips
sipping Fundy streams.
      Why can I not depart from you
like any proud, prodigal son,
ignoring your eyes'
Black Baptist churches?
What keeps me from easy going?
      Mother, is it your death
I fear
or my life?

Sierra Leonia

Tendebantque manus ripae ulterioris amore.
— *Virgil*

To Syl Cheney-Coker

I have my Nova Scotian madness. — Cheney-Coker

      Though under foreign stars I've dreamt too much,
I have my Nova Scotian madness still:
A war-raw, blazing, shipwreck history,
Translated into dark chanties by rum —
"Barbara Allan," "The Nova Scotian Song" —
Moaned dreams that *she* might "heave a sigh for me"
And be my Black Loyalist madonna. . . .
      Dear Syl, O poet-compatriot, I've seized
My birthright — Howe's parliamentary tradition!
      I remember it, even in exile,
Among a strange people, their bank tower gods —
The whited sepulchres of *Republika*,
Where moneyed government holds all power,
And history burns in the cop-cleared streets,
Fooling crass tyrants with dreams that they're God. . . .
O Nova Scotian-Sierra Leonean,
I crave revolution! Flood the stock exchange!
      I have my Nova Scotian madness, Syl.
I wander, exiled, but prize it still.

Journey and Arrival

    Makers risk mystery, masks,
and lone-range, lance,
fording metrical rivers,
crossing prose plains,
to home at last in *Truth* —
found, mapped, and left unsettled
under stars stars stars.
    Inconsequential is the end,
the destination:
mere, public evidence
of the private compass,
the actual but hidden —
the acting but still —
vision and revision.

Discography

Gil Scott-Heron, *Secrets*, Arista, 1978.
John Surman, *Upon Reflection*, ECM, 1979.
Miles Davis, *The Man with the Horn*, CBS, 1980.
Narciso Yepes, *Jeux interdits*, Musidisc, 1981.
Glenn Gould, *Bach: The Goldberg Variations*, CBS, 1982
Anthony Braxton, *Four Compositions*, Black Saint, 1983.
Prince, *Purple Rain*, Warner, 1984.
Sade, *Diamond Life*, Portrait, 1985.
Faith Nolan, *Africville*, Multicultural Women In Concert, 1986.
Gipsy Kings, *Gipsy Kings*, Trans-Canada Disq, 1987.
Four the Moment, *We're Still Standing*, JAM, 1988.
Miles Davis, *Amandla*, Warner, 1989.
Juliette Greco, *Je suis comme je suis*, Phillips, 1990.
Mecano, *Aidalai*, BMG-Espagne, 1991.
Wynton Marsalis Septet, *Blue Interlude*, Columbia, 1992.
Zbigniew Preisner, *Trois Couleurs: Blue*, Virgin-France, 1993.

George Elliott Clarke was born in 1960 in Windsor Plains, Nova Scotia. His other books are *Saltwater Spirituals and Deeper Blues* (Pottersfield Press, 1983) and *Whylah Falls* (Polestar Books, 1990). *Provençal Songs*, a booklet, appeared in 1993. Recently he edited *Fire on the Water* (Pottersfield Press, 1991-1992), a two-volume anthology of Balck Nova Scotian (Africadian) writing. The poems in *Lush Dreams, Blue Exile* were conjured between 1978 and 1993 in Halifax, Québec City, Ottawa, Kingston, Toronto, Kitchener-Waterloo and Banff. Clarke teaches African-American literature at Duke University, Durham, North Carolina.